Specific Skill Series

Following Directions

Richard A. Boning

Fifth Edition

SRA/McGraw-Hill
Columbus, Ohio

Cover, Back Cover, ZEFA/Germany/The Stock Market

SRA/McGraw-Hill

A Division of The **McGraw·Hill** *Companies*

Printed in the United States of America.

Send all inquiries to:
    SRA/McGraw-Hill
    8787 Orion Place
    Columbus, OH 43240-4027

ISBN 0-02-687933-6

        6 7 8 9 IMP 00 99

To the Teacher

PURPOSE:
FOLLOWING DIRECTIONS is designed to develop skill in reading, understanding, and following instructions and directions. Proficiency in this basic skill is essential for success in every school subject and in nonacademic activities as well.

FOR WHOM:
The skill of FOLLOWING DIRECTIONS is developed through a series of books spanning ten levels (Picture, Preparatory, A, B, C, D, E, F, G, H). The Picture Level is for pupils who have not acquired a basic sight vocabulary. The Preparatory Level is for pupils who have a basic sight vocabulary but are not yet ready for the first-grade-level book. Books A through H are appropriate for pupils who can read on levels one through eight, respectively. **The use of the *Specific Skill Series Placement Test* is recommended to determine the appropriate level.**

THE NEW EDITION:
The fifth edition of the *Specific Skill Series* maintains the quality and focus that has distinguished this program for more than 25 years. A key element central to the program's success has been the unique nature of the reading selections. Nonfiction pieces about current topics have been designed to stimulate the interest of students, motivating them to use the comprehension strategies they have learned to further their reading. To keep this important aspect of the program intact, a percentage of the reading selections have been replaced in order to ensure the continued relevance of the subject material.

In addition, a significant percentage of the artwork in the program has been replaced to give the books a contemporary look. The cover photographs are designed to appeal to readers of all ages.

SESSIONS:
Short practice sessions are the most effective. It is desirable to have a practice session every day or every other day, using a few units each session.

SCORING:
Pupils should record their answers on the reproducible worksheets. The worksheets make scoring easier and provide uniform records of the pupils' work. Using worksheets also avoids consuming the exercise books.

It is important for pupils to know how well they are doing. For this reason, units should be scored as soon as they have been completed. Then a discussion can be held in which pupils justify their choices. (The Integrated Language Activities, many of which are open-ended, do not lend themselves to an objective score; thus there are no answer keys for these pages.)

GENERAL INFORMATION ON *FOLLOWING DIRECTIONS*:

FOLLOWING DIRECTIONS focuses attention on four types of directions. The *testing and drilling* directions are like those in most textbooks and workbooks. Mastery of this type, so vital to school success, is stressed throughout FOLLOWING DIRECTIONS. The second type of direction is found in science books and involves *experimenting*. Such material requires the reader to find an answer to a problem or provides the reader with an example of practical application of a principle.

The third type of direction, *assembling*, deals with parts or ingredients and the order and way in which they are put together. Here the purpose is to make or create, rather than to solve a problem or demonstrate a principle.

Directions which tell how to do something are *performing* directions. They accent the steps in learning to do something new. The focus is on the performance rather than on the product.

SUGGESTED STEPS:

On levels A-H, pupils read the information above the first line. Then they answer the questions *below* this line. (Pupils are *not* to respond in writing to information *above* the first line; they are only to study it. Pupils should not write or mark anything in this book.) On the Picture Level, pupils tell if a picture correctly follows the directions. On the Preparatory Level, pupils tell which picture out of two correctly follows the directions.

Additional information on using FOLLOWING DIRECTIONS with pupils will be found in the **Specific Skill Series Teacher's Manual**.

RELATED MATERIALS:

Specific Skill Series Placement Tests, which enable the teacher to place pupils at their appropriate levels in each skill, are available for the Elementary (Pre-1–6) and Midway (4–8) grade levels.

About This Book

Following directions is like trying to find your way with a map. If you follow the directions correctly, you will get where you want to go. If you make mistakes, you will get lost.

Reading directions is different from reading a story. Directions should be read slowly and carefully. If you do not understand something, read it again. Ask yourself questions like these: What do the directions tell me to do? Do I understand all the words in the directions? Should I do one thing before I do something else?

When you are following directions, follow them in the right order. Look for important words, such as *top*, *bottom*, *right*, and *left*.

In this book, you will read four different kinds of directions. Some are like the directions you find on tests and in workbooks. Some tell you how to do experiments. Some tell you how to make things. Some tell you how to do things, such as play a game.

After you read each set of directions, you will answer questions about the directions. One question is about what the directions are for. Others are about details in the directions. The last question makes you think about the directions. Sometimes, you will see how someone followed the directions. Then you will answer the question, "Is this right?" Choose **Yes** if the directions were followed correctly. Choose **No** if the directions were not followed correctly.

DIRECTIONS

Fly a kite in an open spot far from electric power lines. Never use metal wire or wet string. If your kite gets caught in a power line or in tree branches near a power line, don't try to get it down. Instead, call your electric power company.

---

1. This tells you to fly a kite in—

   (A) an open spot

   (B) a busy city

   (C) the water

---

2. Never use metal wire or—

   (A) wet string

   (B) red ribbon

   (C) rubber bands

---

3. A kite caught in or near power lines should be—

   (A) left alone

   (B) pulled loose

   (C) shot at

---

4. You should call your—

   (A) fire department

   (B) police department

   (C) electric power company

DIRECTIONS

Below you will find a very short story. The sentences are not in the right order. Put numbers in front of the sentences to show the right order.

_____ A dancer spun round and round.

_____ The dancer bowed as the curtain closed.

_____ The curtain opened.

1. You are asked to find the—
   - (A) dancer
   - (B) sentence
   - (C) right order

2. You are to look at a story that is very—
   - (A) funny
   - (B) short
   - (C) sad

3. Before each sentence put a—
   - (A) letter
   - (B) number
   - (C) line

4. Is it right? (A) Yes (B) No

   L A dancer spun round and round.

   Q The dancer bowed as the curtain closed.

   B The curtain opened.

DIRECTIONS

Like children, cats do not always want to take medicine. Here is a way to get cats to swallow some. First, measure out the medicine. Then pour the medicine on their fur. Cats are neat, so they will lick it right off.

1. These directions show how to get cats to—

    (A) clean themselves

    (B) obey you

    (C) take medicine

2. You are to put the medicine—

    (A) in a spoon

    (B) in a dish

    (C) on the cat

3. It is clear that most cats—

    (A) do not like medicine

    (B) like medicine

    (C) are not like children

4. Cats will usually lick medicine from—

    (A) a dropper

    (B) a spoon

    (C) their fur

DIRECTIONS

See if you can tell the difference between a sentence and a part of a sentence. Put an **X** in front of the words below that are complete sentences.

_____ **Could not be found.**

_____ **Sat down near me.**

_____ **We went to the store.**

_____ **The children waved to us.**

---

1. You are getting practice in—
    (A) **spelling words**
    (B) **recognizing sentences**
    (C) **using capitals**

2. The groups of words you choose should—
    (A) **not be sentences**
    (B) **be sentences**
    (C) **be parts of sentences**

3. The correct answer must have—
    (A) **an X**
    (B) **a circle**
    (C) **a check mark**

4. Is it right?   (A) **Yes**   (B) **No**

_____ **Could not be found.**

_____ **Sat down near me.**

✓ **We went to the store.**

✓ **The children waved to us.**

DIRECTIONS

Look at each pair of words. Decide which of the two words comes first in alphabetical order. Put a line under it.

meant	rabbit	high
number	leaf	kettle
west	garage	candle
trunk	basket	donkey

1. You are asked to decide the order of—
    (A) **each pair of words**
    (B) **all fifty words**
    (C) **just the first two words**

2. In order to follow these directions, you must know how to—
    (A) **count to twenty**
    (B) **alphabetize words**
    (C) **sound out the letters**

3. Your answer must be—
    (A) **checked**
    (B) **underlined**
    (C) **circled**

4. Is it right? (A) **Yes** (B) **No**

<u>meant</u>	rabbit	<u>high</u>
number	<u>leaf</u>	kettle
west	garage	<u>candle</u>
<u>trunk</u>	<u>basket</u>	donkey

DIRECTIONS

Read the four statements below. If a statement is true, write a **T** on the line. If it is false, write **F**.

_____ Sandwiches are put into lunch boxes.

_____ Babies can read and write.

_____ Snow falls during the winter.

_____ People eat breakfast in the morning.

---

1. You are asked to decide whether statements are—
    - (A) true or false
    - (B) questions
    - (C) sentences

2. Your answer will have a—
    - (A) T or F
    - (B) N or Y
    - (C) T or N

3. The letters must be placed—
    - (A) after the sentences
    - (B) on the lines
    - (C) under the sentences

4. Is it right?   (A) Yes   (B) No

true Sandwiches are put into lunch boxes.

false Babies can read and write.

true Snow falls during the winter.

true People eat breakfast in the morning.

DIRECTIONS

Read each word at the left. Find the same word at the right. Put a line under it.

age.. act............... add............... age.......................

jump.. jar............... jump............ join.......................

house.. house.......... horse........... home....................

---

1. You are to look for a word to the right that is the same as the one on the—
   - (A) left
   - (B) step
   - (C) top

---

2. You are to draw a—
   - (A) letter
   - (B) picture
   - (C) line

---

3. Your mark must be made—
   - (A) under the word
   - (B) over the word
   - (C) in back of the word

---

4. Is it right?   (A) Yes   (B) No

age.. (act.)........... add............... age.......................

jump.. (jar.)........... jump............ join.......................

house.. (house.)....... horse........... home....................

DIRECTIONS

You can put together a toy for your pet that makes music. Run a rubber band through the hole of an empty spool. Tie a small bell at each end. Glue bits of colored wool around the spool. Your pet will make music by rolling and chasing the colorful toy around.

---

1. These directions tell you how to make something for your—

   (A) parents

   (B) pet

   (C) teacher

2. A rubber band is pushed through the hole of a—

   (A) needle

   (B) door

   (C) spool

3. Bells are tied to the rubber band to make—

   (A) weight

   (B) music

   (C) footprints

4. The colored wool makes the toy—

   (A) dark

   (B) bright

   (C) dull

DIRECTIONS

Draw a circle around the word that means the same as the word at the start of the line.

little............................ small.................... big........................ large.................

under.......................... before................. over...................... beneath............

house.......................... pipe...................... home...................... mouse.............

---

1. You are to look for words that—
   - (A) **mean the same**
   - (B) **are opposites**
   - (C) **are long**

---

2. The correct answer should be—
   - (A) **missing**
   - (B) **underlined**
   - (C) **circled**

---

3. The answer should mean the same as the—
   - (A) **first word**
   - (B) **rhyming word**
   - (C) **last word**

---

4. Is it right? (A) **Yes** (B) **No**

little............................ (small).................... big........................ large.................

under.......................... before................. over...................... (beneath)............

house.......................... pipe...................... (home).................... mouse.............

UNIT 10

DIRECTIONS

There are four words in the left-hand column. To the right of each word are two more words. Choose the one that is opposite in meaning to the word at the left. Circle it.

listen	— speak, hear
below	— beside, above
everyone	— lately, nobody
many	— few, some

1. You are to find a word that is—

    (A) the same in meaning
    (B) the opposite in meaning
    (C) very easy

2. You are to choose from—

    (A) two words
    (B) four words
    (C) five words

3. The word you choose must be—

    (A) checked
    (B) circled
    (C) written

4. Is it right?   (A) Yes   (B) No

listen	— speak, hear
below	— beside, above
everyone	— lately, nobody
many	— few, some

15

DIRECTIONS

In each sentence below one of the words is not complete. Look at the letters below the sentence. Find the letter that is missing from the word. Circle it.

Here is a p.....n to write with.

a   e   r

Isn't the s.....n hot today?

u   s   i

---

1. You are asked to find the—
   - (A) complete story
   - (B) missing letter
   - (C) missing words

2. You must look at the—
   - (A) whole alphabet
   - (B) letters under the sentence
   - (C) numbers to the right

3. You are asked to make a—
   - (A) circle
   - (B) line
   - (C) box

4. Is it right?   (A) Yes   (B) No

Here is a p.....n to write with.

a   (e)   r

Isn't the s.....n hot today?

(u)   s   i

UNIT 12

DIRECTIONS

You can make a pretty box to keep little things in. Cover a small box with black paper. Use a paper punch to press out tiny circles of colored paper. Paste the circles on the black paper in a pleasing way. Paint two coats of clear finish over the box.

1. You will need a box, black paper, colored paper, clear finish, and—

    (A) a pencil

    (B) thread

    (C) a paper punch

2. The box is to be covered with—

    (A) black paper

    (B) cloth

    (C) gold

3. The paper punch is used to—

    (A) make a notebook

    (B) make tiny circles

    (C) draw dots

4. After the circles are pasted on, the box is covered with—

    (A) red paint

    (B) black paper

    (C) clear finish

A. Exercising Your Skill

Directions give you steps to follow. The steps should be given in the right order.

The directions below tell you how to make an ocean in a bottle. The directions are not in the right order. On your paper, write the steps in the right order.

Fill half the bottle with water.

Find a big, clear bottle with a twist top.

Put blue vegetable dye in the water.

Close the bottle.

Tip the bottle on its side to make waves.

Add cooking oil on top of the blue water until the bottle is full.

B. Expanding Your Skill

Talk about the directions above with your class. Answer these questions:

- What things do you need if you want to make an ocean in a bottle?
- What do you do first?
- What do you do next?
- What other things do you do?
- What is the last thing that you do?
- What things might happen if you did not follow the steps in the right order?

C. Exploring Language

How could the directions for the ocean in a bottle have been written to make them easy to follow? One way is to number the steps. Another way is to use time order words. Here are some time order words that the writer could have used:

first	next	then	now
second	finally	last	after
before	third	when	later

On your paper, rewrite the directions for making an ocean in a bottle. Add time order words to the directions.

D. Expressing Yourself

Do one of these things.

1. Gather the materials for making an ocean in a bottle. Follow the directions carefully. Explain to your classmates what you are doing.

2. Look through how-to books to find something you would like to make. First, gather the materials you will need. Read the directions carefully. Follow the steps in order. When you are finished, explain to someone else how you made it.

3. Think about something you know how to make. Write directions for making this thing. You may want to draw pictures to go with your directions. Give your directions to a classmate. See if your classmate can follow the directions.

DIRECTIONS

At the top of each column is a word that heads a group of words. The words below it may or may not belong in the group. Decide which words belong in the group. Circle only those that have something to do with the head word.

FOOD	PLANTS	ANIMALS
silver	sentence	giraffe
potatoes	tree	different
cabbage	rose	zebra

1. You are to find words that belong to each—
   - **(A) group**
   - **(B) paragraph**
   - **(C) sentence**

2. The words in each group must have something to do with the—
   - **(A) last word**
   - **(B) head word**
   - **(C) story**

3. You are to show your answers with a—
   - **(A) circle**
   - **(B) line**
   - **(C) picture**

4. Is it right?   **(A) Yes**   **(B) No**

FOOD	PLANTS	ANIMALS
silver	sentence	★ giraffe
★ potatoes	★ tree	different
★ cabbage	★ rose	★ zebra

UNIT 14

DIRECTIONS

There are three words on each line. Two of the three belong together. Put an **X** on the word that does not belong.

.... eye.......................... ear........................... tent........................

.... milk......................... cow........................... book.......................

.... blue......................... school....................... red.........................

.... sleep....................... run........................... bed........................

---

1. You are to find a word on each line that—
    - (A) sounds the same
    - (B) does not belong
    - (C) means the same

2. On each line there are—
    - (A) three words
    - (B) two words
    - (C) five words

3. Your answer is to be marked with—
    - (A) a circle
    - (B) an X
    - (C) a star

4. Is it right?　(A) Yes　(B) No

.... eye.......................... ear........................... ~~tent~~........................

.... milk......................... cow........................... ~~book~~.......................

.... blue......................... ~~school~~....................... red.........................

.... sleep....................... ~~run~~........................... bed........................

DIRECTIONS

Read each group of words below. Do they describe something you can hear or something you can taste? Put an X in the box to the right under the correct heading.

	HEAR	TASTE
a door slam		
an apple pie		
a phone ring		
chicken soup		

1. You are to choose words that describe something you can—
   - (A) hear or taste
   - (B) see or touch
   - (C) hear or see

2. To show the answer, you must use—
   - (A) an X
   - (B) a line
   - (C) a circle

3. Your answer must be placed under the—
   - (A) sentence
   - (B) dots
   - (C) correct heading

4. Is it right?   (A) Yes   (B) No

	HEAR	TASTE
a door slam		X
an apple pie	X	
a phone ring		X
chicken soup	X	

DIRECTIONS

Read the parts of the sentences below. Make each one into a whole sentence. Write your complete sentence on the line below each sentence part.

went to school

_____

in our car

_____

1. You are asked to make—
    - (A) whole sentences
    - (B) sentence parts
    - (C) capital letters

2. You have been given two—
    - (A) letters
    - (B) whole thoughts
    - (C) parts of sentences

3. You are asked to—
    - (A) number each sentence
    - (B) write each sentence
    - (C) check each sentence

4. Is it right?   (A) Yes   (B) No

went to school

The children went to school on the bus.

in our car

We took a long trip in our car.

DIRECTIONS

Read each sentence below. Notice the word that is underlined. Then look at the words to the right of each sentence. Put a star in front of the word that means the same, or almost the same, as the underlined word.

Everyone <u>rushed</u> to the parade.   walked   ran

I <u>lifted</u> the cat into the air.   raised   dropped

At last the game was <u>over</u>.   started   finished

---

1. You are asked to find words that—
   - (A) mean the opposite
   - (B) mean the same
   - (C) start the same

2. You are to find the meaning of the—
   - (A) circled word
   - (B) underlined word
   - (C) first word

3. Your answers must have a—
   - (A) circle around
   - (B) star in front
   - (C) line under

4. Is it right?   (A) Yes   (B) No

Everyone <u>rushed</u> to the parade.   walked   ★ ran

I <u>lifted</u> the cat into the air.   ★ raised   dropped

At last the game was <u>over</u>.   started   ★ finished

UNIT 18

Study the sentences below. In each sentence draw a line under the word that tells **who**. Then circle the word that says **how**.

We talked quietly.

You ran quickly.

The children sang softly.

---

1. First, look for words that tell—
    (A) when
    (B) who
    (C) where

2. Then, look for words that tell—
    (A) why
    (B) how
    (C) what

3. Your answers must be—
    (A) underlined and circled
    (B) underlined and checked
    (C) colored and circled

4. Is it right?   (A) Yes   (B) No

We talked quietly.

You ran quickly.

The children sang softly.

DIRECTIONS

What happens to plants if they do not get light? You can find out by doing this experiment.

EXPERIMENT

Use two plants. Water both of them well. Cover one plant with a bag. Do not cover the other plant. After five days, take off the bag. Look at the plants.

1. You are to find out what happens when plants do not get—
   (A) water
   (B) light
   (C) heat

2. Give both plants plenty of—
   (A) sand
   (B) salt
   (C) water

3. Over one plant you must put a—
   (A) book
   (B) bag
   (C) egg

4. You are to look at the plants after—
   (A) a day
   (B) a year
   (C) five days

DIRECTIONS

Here is how to give medicine to your dog. Raise its head upward. Pull its lower lip out and upward. Then pour in the medicine. Hold its jaws tightly until it swallows. Be careful not to get your fingers in the dog's mouth. If your dog has to take a pill, roll the pill in peanut butter. The dog will gulp it down eagerly.

1. These directions tell you how to—

    (A) train your dog

    (B) keep your dog healthy

    (C) give your dog medicine

2. To keep the pill out of sight—

    (A) put it in a box

    (B) wrap it in paper

    (C) cover it with peanut butter

3. Before you pull the dog's lip out and upward,—

    (A) put in the peanut butter

    (B) raise its head

    (C) pour in the medicine

4. Before you hold its jaws tightly,—

    (A) pull out its tongue

    (B) pour in the medicine

    (C) lower its head

DIRECTIONS

Do you want to make a tent? Get a long pole. Hammer it into the ground leaving three or more feet sticking up above the ground. Tie an open umbrella near the top of the pole. Cover the umbrella with a big cloth.

---

1. This tells you how to make—

    (A) a pole

    (B) a tent

    (C) an umbrella

2. You are asked to hammer a—

    (A) nail

    (B) table

    (C) pole

3. The umbrella you use must be—

    (A) closed

    (B) opened

    (C) wet

4. You are to place a big cloth over the—

    (A) ground

    (B) umbrella

    (C) tree

DIRECTIONS

If you get chewing gum on your clothes, here is how to get it off. Place an ice cube against the gum. In a few minutes the gum will no longer be soft and sticky. It will turn hard. Then just pick the gum off your clothing.

1. These directions tell you how to—

    (A) keep your clothes neat

    (B) use ice cubes

    (C) get gum off your clothing

2. You are to make the gum—

    (A) melt

    (B) stick to the cube

    (C) hard

3. The ice cube is to be placed—

    (A) inside the clothes

    (B) in your shoes

    (C) against the gum

4. You are to take off the gum by—

    (A) chewing it

    (B) melting it

    (C) picking it

DIRECTIONS

Letters from one word can sometimes be put in a different order to spell another word. Three names are printed below. In the blanks write the letters of the names in a different order to fit the clues.

ABBY   —a newborn child   _____

LEE   —a fish   _____

MARY   —many soldiers   _____

---

1. You are asked to change the order of the—
   - (A) letters
   - (B) acts
   - (C) stories

2. After each name there are—
   - (A) numbers
   - (B) clues
   - (C) circles

3. You are to write a new word in each—
   - (A) box
   - (B) blank
   - (C) book

4. Is it right?   (A) Yes   (B) No

ABBY   —a newborn child   **BABY**

LEE   —a fish   **EEL**

MARY   —many soldiers   **ARMY**

DIRECTIONS

Here are some ways to remember the names of people you meet: (1) Listen when the name is said. (2) Learn how to spell the name. (3) Say something about the name. This makes you use it. (4) Be sure to say the name when you say good-bye.

1. When the name is said,—

     (A) listen

     (B) wave

     (C) stamp

2. Find out how the name is—

     (A) spelled

     (B) folded

     (C) practiced

3. Talk about the name, so the name is—

     (A) forgotten

     (B) used

     (C) overlooked

4. Say the name when you say—

     (A) good-bye

     (B) bah

     (C) golly

A. Exercising Your Skill

Directions may tell you how to mark an answer. These are some directions you may be asked to follow:

number the sentences	put an **X** on
write **T** for <u>true</u>	draw a line under
draw a circle around	write a complete sentence

Number your paper from 1 to 4. Read each set of directions below. See if the directions were followed. On your paper next to each number, write *yes* if the directions were followed. Write *no* if they were not followed.

1. Draw a line under the word in the sentence that tells **who**.
   You <u>ran</u> quickly.

2. Put an **X** on the word that does not belong.
   eye   ear   ~~book~~   nose

3. Circle the words that mean the same.
   (little) big (small) cold

4. Number these words in ABC order.
   _1_ horse   _3_ cow   _2_ pig

B. Expanding Your Skill

Look through this book and other school books. Read the directions for marking answers. What are some of the different ways of marking answers? Some directions might tell you to **circle the letter beside the answer**. Others might tell you to **write the answer on your paper**. List four other ways to mark answers. Compare your list with others in your class. How many different ways to mark answers have you found?

C. Exploring Language

The set of directions below is not complete. Copy the directions onto your paper. Then finish the directions. You may use some of the direction words from Parts A and B. You will use more than one word for some of the blanks.

> First, take a sheet of drawing paper. At the top of the paper, draw two _____ . On one _____ , _____ . At the bottom of the paper, draw three _____ . _____ next to each _____ . Finally, _____ .

Trade papers with a friend. Follow the directions your friend wrote. See how different your friend's directions are.

D. Expressing Yourself

Do one of these things.

1. Think about the rules you have learned for following directions. Work with your class to make a chart titled "Following Directions." On the chart, list the rules to follow. List them in the right order.

2. As a class, come up with a list of directions that a new student in your class should follow. What do you do first when you come into the room? Where do you put your things? List everything you think a new student should know. When you have listed everything you can think of, choose the five most important things on the list. List them in an order that makes sense.

3. Work with a partner. Take turns giving each other directions. You might give directions for drawing a picture or making something. Try to follow your partner's directions correctly.

DIRECTIONS

Here are some word squares. Circle the squares that spell the same word across and down.

a	p	e
p	e	a
e	a	r

b	a	g
t	o	e
s	e	e

s	a	w
a	c	e
w	e	b

1. This unit shows you word—

    (A) sentences

    (B) squares

    (C) books

2. To outline the right answers, you must use—

    (A) circles

    (B) squares

    (C) cones

3. You are to look for the same words going—

    (A) across and down

    (B) through the center

    (C) up and down

4. Is it right?   (A) Yes   (B) No

a	p	e
p	e	a
e	a	r

b	a	g
t	o	e
s	e	e

s	a	w
a	c	e
w	e	b

UNIT 26

DIRECTIONS

A sentence is a group of words that make a complete thought. The groups of words below are not sentences. Add some words to each group to make it into a sentence. Begin each sentence with a capital letter and put a period or question mark at the end.

the door

_____

to the school

_____

1. You are asked to make—
    - **(A) complete sentences**
    - **(B) parts of sentences**
    - **(C) parts of words**

2. To each word group, you need to—
    - **(A) take away words**
    - **(B) add words**
    - **(C) find little words**

3. Each sentence must have a period or question mark and a—
    - **(A) name**
    - **(B) comma**
    - **(C) capital letter**

4. Is it right?   **(A) Yes**   **(B) No**

the door

Please close the door.

to the school

I went to the school.

35

UNIT 27

DIRECTIONS

Look at the three words on each line below. Find a word on each line that has one of these sounds—**un, an, en**. Draw a circle around it.

.... then.......................... this.......................... cat..........................

.... fun.......................... him.......................... fox..........................

.... call.......................... top.......................... can..........................

---

1. You are to look for words with—
   - (A) un, an, en
   - (B) it, at, et
   - (C) all, ell, ill

2. The right answers must be—
   - (A) circled
   - (B) underlined
   - (C) crossed out

3. On each line there is—
   - (A) one right answer
   - (B) two right answers
   - (C) no right answer

4. Is it right?   (A) Yes   (B) No

.... then.......................... this.......................... (cat)..........................

.... fun.......................... (him).......................... fox..........................

.... (call).......................... top.......................... can..........................

DIRECTIONS

A part of a sentence can answer the question **where**. The word **where** makes you think of a place. Find the part that tells **where** in each of the two sentences below. Draw a line under it.

We went to the movies in the afternoon.

There, in the middle of the road, sat a turtle.

---

1. You are asked to find—
   - **(A) reason words**
   - **(B) time words**
   - **(C) place words**

2. The words about a place answer the question—
   - **(A) how**
   - **(B) when**
   - **(C) where**

3. The answer should be—
   - **(A) circled**
   - **(B) underlined**
   - **(C) checked**

4. Is it right? **(A) Yes** **(B) No**

We went to the movies <u>in the afternoon</u>.

There, in the middle of the road, <u>sat a turtle</u>.

UNIT 29

DIRECTIONS

Do you want to have a turtle race? Get your friends to line up with their bikes at a starting line. On a signal they must ride as slowly as possible to the finish line. The rider who gets there last wins. Anyone who touches a foot to the ground during the race is out.

---

1. This tells you how to play—

   (A) horse race
   (B) boat race
   (C) turtle race

2. Those in the race ride on—

   (A) cars
   (B) horses
   (C) bikes

3. After hearing a signal, the riders go—

   (A) slowly
   (B) quickly
   (C) swiftly

4. The last person to get to the finish line—

   (A) loses
   (B) wins
   (C) finds

DIRECTIONS

If someone tells you there is no more toothpaste in the tube, do this trick. Let hot water run on the "empty" tube for several minutes. Then ask the person to squeeze the tube. Like magic, there will be enough for a last brushing.

---

1. This tells you how to—

    (A) brush your teeth

    (B) find more toothpaste

    (C) use hot water

2. You are to put the tube under—

    (A) the sink

    (B) hot water

    (C) cold water

3. After the tube is put under water, it is to be—

    (A) squeezed

    (B) thrown away

    (C) shaken

4. When the tube is squeezed,—

    (A) no paste will come out

    (B) the tube will be empty

    (C) the last of the paste will come out

DIRECTIONS

Do things float better in salt water?

EXPERIMENT

Put an egg into a glass. Then pour in fresh water. The egg will stay on the bottom of the glass. Now pour salt into the water. The egg will rise to the surface.

1. You are to find out what happens to things that float in—

    (A) salt water

    (B) air

    (C) a glass

2. Before you pour in the salt,—

    (A) put in an egg

    (B) take out the egg

    (C) pour out the water

3. When a boat is taken from fresh water and placed in the ocean, it will float—

    (A) worse

    (B) better

    (C) the same

4. In the Great Salt Lake, which is much saltier than the ocean, it is almost impossible to—

    (A) sink

    (B) float

    (C) walk

DIRECTIONS

All but one of the letters of the alphabet are printed below. Look at them carefully. Write the letter that has been left out on the line.

ABCDEFGHIJKLMNOPRSTUVWXYZ

_____

---

1. You are asked to find out which letter is—
   - **(A) first**
   - **(B) missing**
   - **(C) last**

2. You are to write—
   - **(A) the alphabet**
   - **(B) the missing letter**
   - **(C) part of a sentence**

3. You are to write your answer—
   - **(A) at the start**
   - **(B) in the middle**
   - **(C) on the line**

4. Is it right?   **(A) Yes**   **(B) No**

ABCDEFGHIJKLMNOPRSTUVWXYZ

_____O_____

DIRECTIONS

You can make leaf creatures. Find different kinds of leaves. Place the leaves on paper and outline their shapes with a crayon or pen. Let your imagination go wild as you add ears, noses, eyes, mouths, tails, and legs.

1. This tells you how to make leaf—

    (A) pods

    (B) creatures

    (C) soup

2. You are to find leaves that are—

    (A) different

    (B) matching

    (C) the same

3. To outline leaf shapes, use a pen or—

    (A) wire

    (B) crayon

    (C) needle

4. The leaf shapes will turn into strange creatures as you add—

    (A) body parts

    (B) funny names

    (C) word parts

DIRECTIONS

To hammer a nail, hold the hammer in the hand you use most. Do not hold it tightly near the head. Use the thumb and first two fingers of your other hand to steady the nail. Give a few gentle taps with the hammer until the nail stays in by itself. Take away your fingers. Then drive the nail with harder blows until it goes in all the way.

1. The hand you use most should—

    (A) **hold the nail**

    (B) **hold the hammer**

    (C) **touch your hand**

2. Steady the nail with—

    (A) **the thumb and first two fingers**

    (B) **your teeth**

    (C) **the hammer**

3. A few easy taps will keep the nail from—

    (A) **making a hole**

    (B) **going in**

    (C) **falling out**

4. After you take away your fingers, hit the nail—

    (A) **from the side**

    (B) **harder**

    (C) **softer**

DIRECTIONS

Look at the two rows of words below. Each word in the first column means the same as a word in the second column. Draw lines between the words that mean the same.

big	**large**
fast	**small**
little	**quick**

1. You must find the words that—
    - **(A) mean the same**
    - **(B) look the same**
    - **(C) are not alike**

2. You are to look at the words in—
    - **(A) sentences**
    - **(B) two columns**
    - **(C) one column**

3. The words must have lines—
    - **(A) under them**
    - **(B) between them**
    - **(C) over them**

4. Is it right?   **(A) Yes**   **(B) No**

(big)	(large)
(fast)	(small)
(little)	(quick)

DIRECTIONS

Here is an experiment which will help you learn about the top, or surface, of water.

EXPERIMENT

Fill a dish with water. Carefully place a dry needle across a fork. Lower the fork to the top of the water in the dish. Let the needle gently roll off the fork. Watch closely and try to answer these questions: Is the surface of the water like skin? Is it strong? Is the water bent? What happens to the needle?

1. You are to do an experiment to find out about—
   - **(A) running water**
   - **(B) the surface of water**
   - **(C) drinking water**

2. You are to put the water—
   - **(A) on the needle**
   - **(B) on your skin**
   - **(C) in a dish**

3. When you put the needle on the fork, it must be—
   - **(A) sharp**
   - **(B) dry**
   - **(C) threaded**

4. If you watch closely, you will be able to answer questions about—
   - **(A) what happens**
   - **(B) what splashes**
   - **(C) the fork**

DIRECTIONS

You can have an insect zoo. When you find an insect you want to study, put it with some grass and dirt into a clear glass bowl. Place waxed paper over the top and keep it tight with a rubber band. Punch some air holes in the paper. After watching the insect for a day or two, let it go.

1. These directions tell you how to make—

    (A) an apartment

    (B) a fishbowl

    (C) an insect zoo

2. The insect is put into a glass bowl for—

    (A) worry

    (B) study

    (C) repair

3. Holes are punched in the waxed paper top to give the insect—

    (A) warmth

    (B) light

    (C) air

4. After a day or two, the insect should be set—

    (A) free

    (B) upside down

    (C) on fire

DIRECTIONS

Each word below can be made into a new word by adding an ending. Make a whole new word out of each one by adding an **ing**. Write the new word on the line.

play ——————————   swing ——————————

call ——————————   jump ——————————

1. You are to make a new word by adding—
   - **(A) an ending**
   - **(B) a letter**
   - **(C) five letters**

2. The answer is to be written—
   - **(A) below the words**
   - **(B) on the line**
   - **(C) before the words**

3. You must write the—
   - **(A) "ing" only**
   - **(B) whole new word**
   - **(C) same word**

4. Is it right?   **(A) Yes**   **(B) No**

play _playing_   swing _swinging_

call _calling_   jump _jumping_

A. Exercising Your Skill

Directions give you steps to follow. The steps may be numbered, or they may use words like <u>first,</u> <u>next,</u> and <u>then.</u>

These directions tell you how to make a grid number code. Just read these directions. Don't follow them.

GRID NUMBER CODE

First, draw a grid like the one below. It has five squares across and five squares down. Next, on the outside of the grid, number the squares across the top. These are column numbers. Then number the squares down one side. These are row numbers. After that, write one letter of the alphabet in each square. (Two letters will have to share one square. **Y** and **Z** can go together.)

	1	2	3	4	5
1	A	B	C	D	E
2	F	G	H	I	J
3	K	L	M	N	O
4	P	Q	R	S	T
5	U	V	W	X	YZ

To write a letter using this code, first write a letter's row number. Then write its column number. In this grid, **A** is 11, **B** is 12, and so on.

What words in the directions help you know the order to follow? On your paper, list the words.

B. Expanding Your Skill

Talk with your classmates about your list of direction words. Can you think of other words that could be used to tell time order? Work together to add more words to the list.

C. Exploring Language

Read again the directions for the grid number code on page 48. Use the code to figure out what the message below means. Write the message on your paper.

553551 131134 31151541 11 441513431545 1255
53432445243422 2434 13351415.

Use the code to write your own secret message. Then trade messages with a friend. Try to figure out what your friend's message is.

D. Expressing Yourself

Do one of these things.

1. Find a book of codes in the library. Share the directions for using a code with a friend. Send messages to each other in code.

2. Make up a code of your own. Write a set of directions for using the code. Explain the directions to a friend so that you can trade secret messages.

3. Here is another code. For every letter, use the letter that is just below it.
   A B C D E F G H I J K L M N O P Q R S T U V W X Y Z
   V W X Y Z A B C D E F G H I J K L M N O P Q R S T U
   Write a message using this code.

DIRECTIONS

Do you have mice in your house? Here are some good ways to catch them with a trap. Bait the trap with peanut butter or cheese. Mice find these foods tasty. If you have no peanut butter or cheese, try cotton. Mice like to use it for building their nests.

1. From these directions you have learned that mice—

    (A) **eat anything**

    (B) **have favorite foods**

    (C) **are hardly ever hungry**

2. It is clear that mice often live in—

    (A) **the cold**

    (B) **buildings**

    (C) **trees**

3. You can also be sure that mice—

    (A) **are fast**

    (B) **are neat**

    (C) **build nests for themselves**

4. You have also learned that mice—

    (A) **eat cotton**

    (B) **get tangled up in cotton**

    (C) **use cotton for their nests**

DIRECTIONS

As you read each sentence below, look at the two words to the right of it. One of these words must be used to complete the sentence. Choose the correct word and circle it.

Debbie..................to see Jane.	wanting	wanted
Jeff...............to the store.	walk	walked
Three of the.............came here.	child	children

1. You must choose the word that—
   - (A) is funny
   - (B) fits in
   - (C) is short

2. You are to look at words to the right of each—
   - (A) story
   - (B) picture
   - (C) sentence

3. You are asked to—
   - (A) circle
   - (B) check
   - (C) cross out

4. Is it right? (A) Yes (B) No

Debbie..................to see Jane.	wanting	wanted
Jeff...............to the store.	walk	walked
Three of the.............came here.	child	children

DIRECTIONS

Here are ways to keep a new puppy quiet and happy at night. Put a ticking alarm clock in its box. The ticking will remind the puppy of the beating of its mother's heart. Wrap a hot water bottle in a blanket and place it nearby. It will make the puppy feel warm and protected.

1. From these directions you learn how to—

(A) **run a kennel**

(B) **keep a puppy happy at night**

(C) **take care of a dog**

2. The ticking alarm clock reminds the puppy of—

(A) **its mother's heartbeat**

(B) **its brothers and sisters**

(C) **a cat**

3. A blanket is used to wrap the—

(A) **puppy**

(B) **clock**

(C) **hot water bottle**

4. The puppy will feel as if—

(A) **its mother is nearby**

(B) **the box is crowded**

(C) **it's very noisy**

UNIT 42

DIRECTIONS

Read each of the words below. Think of the number of syllables in each one. If the word has one syllable, write **1** in front of it. If it has two syllables, write **2**.

_____ under   _____ spring   _____ rhyme

_____ matter   _____ pasture   _____ welcome

_____ pilot   _____ sudden   _____ chatter

---

1. You are to figure out the—
   - (A) order of words
   - (B) meaning of words
   - (C) number of syllables

2. Each of the words has either—
   - (A) one or two syllables
   - (B) three or four syllables
   - (C) no syllables

3. You are asked to write the number—
   - (A) in back of the word
   - (B) in front of the word
   - (C) under the word

4. Is it right?   (A) Yes   (B) No

2 under   **1** spring   **1** rhyme

2 matter   **2** pasture   **2** welcome

2 pilot   **2** sudden   **2** chatter

DIRECTIONS

Read each sentence. Write **Yes** if the sentence is true. Write **No** if the sentence is not true.

Children can run. ─────

Coats keep us warm. ─────

Big books can fly. ─────

1. Answer "Yes" or "No" about each—
   - **(A) sentence**
   - **(B) word**
   - **(C) story**

2. Your answer must be—
   - **(A) written**
   - **(B) guessed**
   - **(C) read out loud**

3. Your answer will be "Yes" if the sentence is—
   - **(A) not true**
   - **(B) true**
   - **(C) a word**

4. Is it right?   **(A) Yes**   **(B) No**

   Children can run. _Yes_

   Coats keep us warm. _Yes_

   Big books can fly. _No_

DIRECTIONS

Look at the calendar page. Write the answers to the questions on the lines below.

			MAY			
S	M	T	W	T	F	S
					1	2
3	4	5	6	7	8	9
10	11	12	13	14	15	16
17	18	19	20	21	22	23
24	25	26	27	28	29	30
31						

On which day of the week does the second fall?

_____

What is the date of the last Monday of the month?

_____

---

1. You are asked to answer questions about—

    (A) March

    (B) the calendar page

    (C) years

2. The letters "S, M, T, W, T, F, S," on the calendar stand for—

    (A) a year

    (B) a month

    (C) days of the week

3. The answers should be—

    (A) written

    (B) checked

    (C) circled

4. Is it right?   (A) Yes   (B) No

			MAY			
S	M	T	W	T	F	S
					1	2
3	4	5	6	7	8	9
10	11	12	13	14	15	16
17	18	19	20	21	22	23
24	25	26	27	28	29	30
31						

On which day of the week does the second fall?

Saturday

What is the date of the last Monday of the month?

May 25

DIRECTIONS

Some of the words below describe how something looks. They are called picture words because they help give a clear picture of something. Underline the picture words.

is	green	small
red	and	but
big	are	can

1. You are to look for words that help you—
   - **(A) spell well**
   - **(B) count well**
   - **(C) picture things**

2. Picture words describe how something—
   - **(A) looks**
   - **(B) sounds**
   - **(C) tastes**

3. Your answer must be—
   - **(A) circled**
   - **(B) underlined**
   - **(C) written**

4. Is it right?   **(A) Yes**   **(B) No**

<u>is</u>	green	small
red	<u>and</u>	<u>but</u>
big	<u>are</u>	<u>can</u>

DIRECTIONS

Read the sentences below. Think of the endings that should be added. Circle them.

The children walked slow.......... up the hill.

ish   ly   ing

We were follow.......... the leader.

ed   ing   est

---

1. You are asked to choose—
    - **(A) the first word**
    - **(B) the right sentence**
    - **(C) the right ending**

2. The answer choices are found—
    - **(A) below the sentences**
    - **(B) above the sentences**
    - **(C) beside the sentences**

3. The correct answers should be—
    - **(A) checked**
    - **(B) crossed out**
    - **(C) circled**

4. Is it right?   **(A) Yes**   **(B) No**

The children walked slow.......... up the hill.

ish   ly   (ing)

We were follow.......... the leader.

(ed)   ing   est

DIRECTIONS

Write the answer for each sentence on the line. The answer must be a word with a short **o** sound.

We put the toys into the _____ .

It is very _____ today.

Mother has a new _____ .

---

1. You are to think of—
   - (A) short vowel words
   - (B) long vowel words
   - (C) big words

2. Each answer must be written—
   - (A) in the box
   - (B) on the line
   - (C) in the circle

3. You are asked to write the—
   - (A) vowel "i"
   - (B) word
   - (C) vowel "e"

4. Is it right?   (A) Yes   (B) No

We put the toys into the _box_ .

It is very _hot_ today.

Mother has a new _top_ .

DIRECTIONS

Do you have a rusty knife? Here is how to make the rust disappear. Stick the blade into an onion. Leave it there for an hour. Then take the knife out of the onion and wash the blade. Use a cloth to wipe it dry. Watch the rust come right off!

1. This tells you how to—

    (A) use a knife

    (B) cut onions

    (C) get rid of rust

2. You are to stick the blade into—

    (A) the bread

    (B) the meat

    (C) an onion

3. Before you wash the blade,—

    (A) shine it

    (B) pull it from the onion

    (C) heat it

4. You are to take the knife from the onion after—

    (A) a minute

    (B) a day

    (C) an hour

DIRECTIONS

You can make pretty note cards with dried flowers. Collect some small flowers. Press them in a book for twenty-four hours, or until they are flat. Cut sheets of $8\frac{1}{2}$ by 11-inch paper in half from side to side. Fold each half. Spread glue on the flowers with a toothpick. Place the flowers nicely on the front of each card. Make sure the glue dries. Use the cards for party invitations, writing paper, or cards for special days.

1. You are to collect—
    (A) shells
    (B) flowers
    (C) stamps

2. Cut in half paper that measures—
    (A) $8\frac{1}{2}$ by 11 inches
    (B) $8\frac{1}{2}$ by 14 inches
    (C) 3 by 5 inches

3. Spread the glue with—
    (A) your finger
    (B) a toothpick
    (C) an envelope

4. Be sure that the glue—
    (A) melts
    (B) freezes
    (C) dries

DIRECTIONS

Do you have trouble pulling your rubber boots over your shoes? Put plastic bags over your shoes first. Bread bags are the perfect size. You will find that your boots now slip on easily over the slippery plastic. Your shoes will stay drier too, with their plastic coverings.

1. You are asked to cover your shoes with—

    (A) **leather polish**

    (B) **plastic bags**

    (C) **olive oil**

2. Bread bags are—

    (A) **the perfect size**

    (B) **much too costly**

    (C) **not large enough**

3. Boots will slip on easily over the slippery—

    (A) **ice**

    (B) **plastic**

    (C) **glass**

4. The extra covering will keep your shoes—

    (A) **lighter**

    (B) **looser**

    (C) **drier**

A. Exercising Your Skill

There are different kinds of directions. Some directions are the kind you see in workbooks and on tests. Some directions tell you how to carry out an experiment. Some tell you how to put something together. Still others tell you how to do something, such as play a game.

Read each set of directions below. Think about what the directions are for. Match each set of directions with a title from the box. Write the numbers 1, 2, and 3 on your paper. Next to each number, write the title that fits the directions.

How-to Directions	Experiment Directions	Workbook Directions

1. You can make leaf creatures. Find different kinds of leaves. Place the leaves on paper and outline their shapes with a crayon or pen. Add ears, noses, eyes, mouths, tails, and legs.

2. Look at each pair of words. Decide which of the two words comes first in alphabetical order. Put a line under it.

meant	rabbit	high
number	leaf	kettle

3. Do things float better in salt water? You can find out by putting an egg into a glass. Then pour in fresh water. The egg will stay on the bottom of the glass. Now pour salt into the water. The egg will rise to the surface.

B. Expanding Your Skill

Write a set of clear, easy-to-follow directions for how to draw a big picture of a _____ face. For example, it could be funny, happy, sad, silly, ugly, or scary. Give your directions to a classmate to follow while you follow the directions a classmate gives to you.

C. Exploring Language

Read each of these sets of directions. On your paper, write a title for each set of directions. Your titles should explain what the directions are for. (For example, directions that explain how to wash a dog could have the title "How to Wash a Dog.")

1. Like children, cats do not always want to take medicine. Here is a way to get cats to swallow some. First, measure out the medicine. Then pour the medicine on their fur. Cats are neat, so they will lick it right off.

2. Long ago, people wrote with pictures instead of letters. Here's how you can do it too. If your name is Pat, you can draw a pen for "p," an apple for "a," and a table for "t." Now study your name and remember how it looks in picture writing.

3. You can make a pretty box to keep little things in. Cover a small box with black paper. Use a paper punch to press out tiny circles of colored paper. Paste the circles onto the black paper in a pleasing way. Paint two coats of clear finish over the box.

4. Here is a way to make buds open ahead of time. In the spring, cut some twigs from an apple or cherry tree. Bring the twigs into the house and place them in a jar of water. Watch the buds on the twigs each day to see what happens. Keep a record of what you see happening. Write one or two sentences each day about what you see.

D. Expressing Yourself

Read the directions in Part C for writing your name with pictures. Think of pictures for your name. Write your name in picture writing. Tell why you chose the things you did for each letter of your name.